DISCOVER CATS WITH THE CAT FANCIERS' ASSOCIATION

THE CAT FANCIERS' ASSOCIATION
CFA
SINCE 1906
www.cfa.org

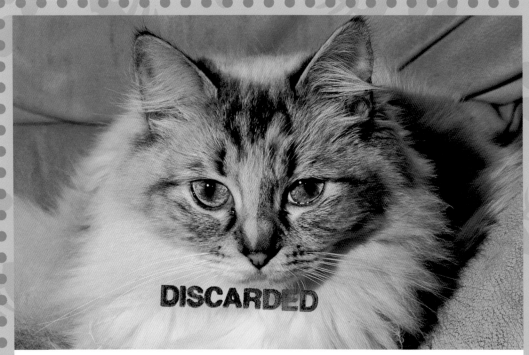

♥ ♥ ♥ ♥ ♥ DISCOVER ♥ ♥ ♥ ♥ ♥
RAGDOLL CATS

Trudy Micco

The Cat Fanciers' Association, Inc.® (CFA™) was founded in 1906 as a not-for-profit association of member clubs and is the world's largest registry of pedigreed cats. CFA's mission is to preserve and promote the pedigreed breeds of cats and to enhance the well-being of ALL cats. CFA promotes education, responsible cat ownership, and proper care to the owners of millions of cats worldwide. CFA and its affiliate clubs work nationally with local shelters, at a grassroots level, to help humanely control homeless and feral cat populations, and to encourage voluntary neutering/spaying of pet cats. To learn more about the Cat Fanciers' Association, the pedigreed breeds of cats, or to find the nearest CFA cat show, visit their Web site at www.cfa.org.

Enslow Elementary, an imprint of Enslow Publishers, Inc.

Enslow Elementary® is a registered trademark of Enslow Publishers, Inc.

Library of Congress Cataloging-in-Publication Data

Micco, Trudy.
  Discover ragdoll cats / Trudy Micco.
    p. cm. — (Discover cats with the cat fanciers' association)
  Includes bibliographical references and index.
  Summary: "Early readers will learn how to care for a ragdoll cat, including breed-specific traits and needs"—Provided by publisher.
  ISBN 978-0-7660-3855-4
  1. Ragdoll cat—Juvenile literature. I. Title.
  SF449.R34M53 2012
  636.8'3—dc22
                                      2011005908

Future editions:
Paperback ISBN 978-1-4644-0113-8
ePUB ISBN 978-1-4645-1020-5
PDF ISBN 978-1-4646-1020-2

Printed in China

012012 Leo Paper Group, Heshan City, Guangdong, China

10 9 8 7 6 5 4 3 2 1

To Our Readers: We have done our best to make sure all Internet Addresses in this book were active and appropriate when we went to press. However, the author and the publisher have no control over and assume no liability for the material available on those Internet sites or on other Web sites they may link to. Any comments or suggestions can be sent by e-mail to comments@enslow.com or to the address on the back cover.

Every effort has been made to locate all copyright holders of material used in this book. If any errors or omissions have occurred, corrections will be made in future editions of this book.

Photo Credits: © Andreas Åkre Solberg, p. 13; © Chris Froome, pp. 1, 6, 17, 23; © Dave Wetzel/Dreamstime.com, p. 19; © Jean Michel Labat/ardea.com, p. 9; © OVIA IMAGES/Alamy, p. 14; Photodisc, p. 22; Shutterstock.com, pp. 3, 11; © wda bravo/Alamy, p. 10; © WJ van den Eijkhof, pp. 5, 18.

Cover Photo: © Jean-Michel Labat/ardea.com (ragdoll sitting).

Enslow Elementary
an imprint of
Enslow Publishers, Inc.
40 Industrial Road
Box 398
Berkeley Heights, NJ 07922
USA
http://www.enslow.com

CONTENTS

IS A RAGDOLL RIGHT FOR YOU?

A ragdoll cat is great if you want a calm and gentle pet. Ragdolls are friendly and may get along with other cats and dogs. Ragdolls are also very smart. You can teach your ragdoll to come when you call his name.

Cats go to the bathroom inside a litter box. You should clean the litter every day. Also, empty the box and wash it once a week.

Some ragdolls and dogs can become best friends!

Kittens are full of energy. Can your family keep up?

A CAT OR KITTEN?

Most people like kittens because they are cute and fun. But kittens can be harder to care for than adult cats. Kittens need more attention from you.

Older cats can be friendlier than kittens at first. Kittens need to get used to being away from their brothers and sisters. Is a kitten or older cat better for your family?

LOVING YOUR RAGDOLL

Ragdolls are very **loyal** and friendly. They act almost like dogs! These cats like to greet you at the door. They will play with you and may follow you around.

Ragdolls will want to sleep with you and be where you are. They enjoy spending time with people.

Your ragdoll will love being with you.

A cat tube is a fun place to hide for your ragdoll.

EXERCISE

Be sure to get special toys for your ragdoll to play with. Playing is exercise for cats. They need exercise to stay healthy.

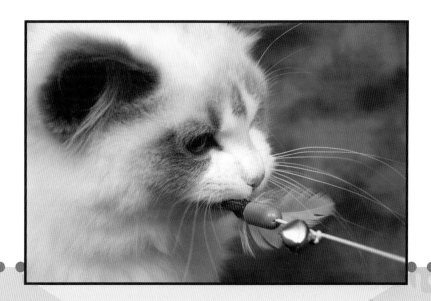

FEEDING YOUR RAGDOLL

There is wet food and dry food made just for cats. Feed and give your cat fresh water every day. A **veterinarian (vet)**, a doctor for animals, can tell you what kind of food and how much to feed your cat.

Be sure to keep your cat's food and water bowls clean. Dirty bowls can make her sick.

Do not give your cat people food. It can make her sick.

Brush his coat to make it fluffy!

GROOMING

Ragdolls have long, soft fur. Comb your cat every day with a special metal comb so the fur does not get **matted**. Bathe your cat once a month to keep the hair clean. Use a special shampoo made just for cats.

Cats scratch on a special post to keep their claws sharp. You can clip their claws once a month. A vet can show you how.

WHAT YOU SHOULD KNOW

Before you bring your new cat home, be sure your home is safe. Some plants are bad for cats.

Cats should not be allowed outside. Cars, mean people, and other animals can hurt them. Cats should stay indoors to stay safe and sound.

Cats enjoy looking out the window when they are indoors.

You will need to take your new cat to the vet for a checkup. He will need shots, called vaccinations, and yearly checkups to keep him healthy. If you think your cat may be sick or hurt, call your vet.

A GOOD FRIEND

Your ragdoll will be a good friend to you for many years. Play with her, feed her, and take good care of her.

NOTE TO PARENTS

You can adopt your cat from a reputable breeder or from a rescue group that specializes in a specific breed. Spaying/neutering your cat prior to six months of age is advised. Neutering and spaying will prevent behavioral problems and many life-threatening diseases and help prevent overpopulation.

To keep your cat safe, keep him indoors. It is also a good idea to microchip your cat, in case he gets lost. A vet will implant a microchip under the skin that contains your contact information, which can then be scanned at a vet's office or animal shelter. Some towns require licenses for cats, so be sure to check with your town clerk. Also, check your home for potential dangers. Some plants and foods are toxic to cats. String can be very dangerous too. Cats like to play with it and sometimes they will eat it, which can cause them to get very sick and require surgery to remove. Ask your vet or visit www.cfa.org for a full list of concerns and for cat-proofing ideas.

Some things you will need before bringing your new cat home:

- **litter box** (Veterinarians recommend more than one in different places in the house.)
- **litter** (There are many brand choices.)
- **water and food bowls** (Use stainless steel, glass, crock, or other nonplastic material.)
- **cat food** (A reputable breeder will recommend a good quality food and how much to feed your cat, or ask your vet. The better quality the food, the healthier the cat, which means fewer trips to the vet's office.)
- **cat bed** (Select something the cat can snuggle into.)
- **special cat toys** (Select safe toys that do not have small parts or string that could come off and injure your cat.)
- **grooming brushes**
- **cat nail clipper** (or a human toenail clipper)
- **scratching posts** (There should be a few in different easily accessible locations in the house to keep the cat from damaging furniture.)
- **carrier** (Make sure your cat can stand up and move around in the carrier as an adult.)

litter box—A special box where cats go to the bathroom.

loyal—Always true to a friend.

matted—Tangled and dirty.

vaccination—A shot that cats need to stay healthy.

veterinarian (vet)—A doctor for animals.

Books

Landau, Elaine. *Ragdolls Are the Best!* Minneapolis,
   Minn.: Lerner Publications, 2011.

Stone, Lynn M. *Ragdoll Cats.* Vero Beach, Fla.:
   Rourke Pub., 2010.

Internet Addresses

The Cat Fanciers' Association: For Kids
<http://kids.cfa.org/>

ASPCA Kids
<http://www.aspca.org/aspcakids/>

INDEX